Snicker the Brownie

...and other stories

Enid Blyton

Snicker the Brownie

...and other stories

Bounty
Books

Published in 2014 by Bounty Books,
a division of Octopus Publishing Group Ltd,
Carmelite House
50 Victoria Embankment
London EC4Y 0DZ
www.octopusbooks.co.uk

An Hachette UK Company
www.hachette.co.uk

Enid Blyton ® Text copyright © 2014 Hodder & Stoughton Ltd.
Illustrations copyright © 2014 Octopus Publishing Group Ltd.
Layout copyright © 2014 Octopus Publishing Group Ltd.

Illustrated by Valerie Ewens and Brian Hoskin.

ISBN: 978-0-75372-672-3

A CIP catalogue record for this book is available from the
British Library.

Printed and bound in the United Kingdom

3 5 7 9 10 8 6 4

CONTENTS

1

Peter's Noah's Ark

Peter had a lovely playhouse at the bottom of the garden. He kept all his toys there, his soldiers, his fortress, his teddy bear, his books and his beautiful Noah's ark with all its animals and birds.

Just outside the playhouse was a little stream, and Peter often used to sail his big boat, his two little boats and his steamer there. He had great fun.

One day his cousin John came to ask if he would go to spend the night with him, and bring all his boats and his steamer.

'I've got a big pond in my garden,' said John. 'We'll sail our boats and have a splendid time.'

So Peter went to his playhouse and

took all his boats. Then he shut the door and off he went with John. The toys felt rather sad, for they knew that no one would play with them that day.

'I do hate it when Peter goes off and leaves us,' said the bear. 'There's nothing much to do. Toys never have adventures like boys and girls. We just stay here and do nothing unless Peter plays with us. Oh, I would like an adventure, wouldn't you?'

'Rather!' cried all the soldiers.

Mr and Mrs Noah looked out of the ark.

'Perhaps one day we shall all have a exciting adventure,' they said.

'Pooh!' said everyone, rudely. 'You're not likely to have adventures with your silly old ark!'

Mr and Mrs Noah said no more. They knew they were old-fashioned, and they often felt hurt when the other toys laughed at their wooden ark.

But that night an adventure really did come to the toys! For just about midnight they heard a great shouting outside, and woke up in a fright. Then someone came knocking at the playhouse door.

'Open, open, in the name of the King of Fairyland!' cried a voice.

The teddy bear ran across the floor and opened the door. Outside stood an elf, wet through and dripping.

'Oh!' he said. 'Such a dreadful thing

has happened. The King and Queen of Fairyland were going along in their ship down the stream, on a visit to the Prince of Buttercup Land, when suddenly a wind came and blew the ship right over!'

'Good gracious!' cried all the toys in horror. 'Are they drowned?'

'No, nobody's drowned,' said the elf. 'But we're all wet through, and the ship has sunk. We want to know if we can come in here and dry ourselves.'

'Of course,' said the toys. 'Of course! Oh dear, we are so sorry! We will light the fire in the old doll's house and you can dry yourselves there.'

The soldiers ran to the doll's house and opened the front door. They quickly lit the fire in the drawing room, and then one of them started the kitchen fire too, and put a jug of cocoa on the stove to warm.

Soon in came the King and Queen, wet through and shivering. They were delighted to see the bright fire, and very soon they were sitting by it, drying

themselves. Their little elfin servants dried themselves by the kitchen fire, and poured out tiny cups of hot cocoa, which they took to the King and Queen.

'We are very sorry to hear of your sad plight, Your Majesty,' said the teddy bear. 'We wish that you could spend the night in the doll's-house, but unfortunately there are no beds. Peter gave them all to a little friend of his one day when she came to play with him.'

'Dear, dear, what a pity!' said the Queen. 'But I'm afraid we mustn't stop after we have dried ourselves. We must get on with our journey, or the Prince of Buttercup Land will be very much worried about us.'

'Perhaps there is a boat here we might borrow?' said the King.

'Oh, Your Majesty, Peter has taken both his big boat and his little boat to his cousin's,' cried the toys in dismay.

'Well, is there a toy steamer we might have?' asked the King.

'Peter's taken that too!' said the teddy bear. 'Oh, Your Majesty, whatever will you do?'

'Well, really, I don't know,' said the King. 'There is nowhere here we can sleep for the night, and nothing we can continue our voyage in. It is a real puzzle!'

Then suddenly Mr and Mrs Noah walked up to the King and bowed stiffly, for they were made of wood.

'Your Majesties!' they said, politely. 'Would you care to borrow our wooden ark? We can easily turn out all the animals and make it comfortable for you. It is watertight and will float very well indeed.'

'I have sometimes heard of a Noah's ark,' said the King, 'but I have never seen one. Let me look at it. The Queen and I are almost dry now.'

So they walked out of the doll's-house and went to see the Noah's ark. All the toys went too, and most of them were very cross with Mr and Mrs Noah.

'Fancy offering to take the King and Queen in your stupid old ark!' they whispered to Mr Noah. 'Whatever were you thinking of?'

But Mr Noah took no notice. He led the King over to the ark, and the Queen went with Mrs Noah.

'Well!' said the King in surprise. 'So that is a Noah's ark! It looks big enough to take us all quite comfortably, much better than a small boat. It is really very kind of you, Mr Noah, to offer to lend it to us. Would you come with us to steer it? I don't think any of my servants know how to guide an ark.'

'Certainly, certainly,' said Mr Noah, blushing with delight. All the toys were most surprised, and said not a word. The King called his servants and showed them the ark.

'Shall we get in now?' he asked.

'I must first get all the animals out,' said Mr Noah. 'They live there, you know, two of each kind.'

Then he clapped his hands and called to the animals. They all pushed up the lid and looked out to see what was happening.

'Come out!' cried Mr Noah. 'The King and Queen of Fairyland want to borrow the ark for a little while.'

Then out tumbled all the wooden animals, and walked up to the King and Queen two by two and bowed. Their Majesties were delighted, and thought

they had never seen such polite animals before.

'Now, Your Majesty, I'll just borrow a ladder from the toy farm,' said Mr Noah, 'and you and the Queen can climb into the ark. Ho, soldiers, fetch some comfortable chairs from the doll's-house for Their Majesties to sit in!'

The soldiers scurried off and came back with chairs. The bear fetched the ladder from the toy farm, and Mr Noah put it against the side of the ark. In a instant the King and Queen and all their servants were safely inside, sitting on their chairs.

Then ropes were tied to the ark, and the soldiers hauled on them. The ark slid across the floor and out on to the grass. Soon it was by the stream, and then, with a gentle splash, it was launched. All the toys cheered and waved goodbye. The wooden ark animals had marched down to the water in twos, and the King and Queen laughed to see them.

Off sailed the ark down the stream

17

in the moonlight. It went right away to Buttercup Land, and the Prince was full of astonishment to see it.

'Thank you so much,' said the King and Queen to Mr and Mrs Noah. 'We don't know what we should have done without you and the wonderful ark. Please come and see us. We will send you an invitation when we get back to Fairyland.'

Mr and Mrs Noah said goodbye, and guided the ark back home. They were simply delighted to think that they had been able to help Their Majesties. As for all the toys in the playhouse, they couldn't make enough fuss of Mr and Mrs Noah.

'We are sorry we laughed at the ark,' they said. 'Do tell us all about your adventures!' And dear me, when the invitation came from the King and Queen to a moonlight party in Fairyland, for Mr and Mrs Noah and all the wooden animals, what excitement there was! And how envious all the other toys were.

Mr and Mrs Noah didn't need to go in the ark, for the elfin messenger said he could take them by a short cut down the garden path, and along a passage in a hollow oak tree. So off they all went.

Mr and Mrs Noah went first, feeling ever so proud. Then came all the animals in twos. It really was a sight to see! I should love to have gone with them, wouldn't you?

2

The Boy Who Wanted a Pet

There was once a boy called Harry. He had no brothers or sisters, so he was often lonely.

'If I had a dog – or a cat – or even a rabbit in a hutch, it would be something to play with and love,' thought Harry. 'I'll ask Mum again. If I ask her often enough, perhaps she'll say yes.'

So he went to find his mother. 'Mum,' he said, 'I know you always say no – but please this time do say yes! Can I have a puppy?'

'Certainly not,' said his mother. 'It would grow into a noisy, barking dog – and bring mud into the house all the time.'

'Well, can I have a kitten then?' said Harry. 'Do, do say yes to a kitten! It wouldn't bark or bring mud into the house.'

'Perhaps not. But it would grow into a cat, and all cats are thieves,' said his mother. 'It would steal food from the larder and jump up on the table. I know cats!'

'Well, a rabbit, then, Mum – a dear

21

little soft, fluffy rabbit with a woffly nose?' said Harry. 'I would keep it in a cage and look after it myself.'

'You wouldn't look after it,' said his mother. 'You'd get tired of it, and then I should have to see to it, and I'm much too busy. I might even have to make it into a pie.'

Mother was joking, but Harry thought she meant it. He went off without another word. He couldn't, couldn't keep any pet that might be eaten! Well, he would have to do without, that was all.

His mother saw that he was upset, and she called after him. 'Harry! Get out your new little garage and arrange your cars in it. You'll like that. Take it down the garden – it's warm enough in the shed for you to play with it there.'

Harry cheered up. He went into his playroom and fetched his two garages. One was small and old and needed painting. The other was big and brand-new, and would hold all his tiny little cars. It would be fun to change them over from the old garage to the new one.

He carried both garages down to the shed in the garden, and the little cars, too. The winter sun came into the shed and it was nice and warm. Harry began to sort out his cars.

He talked to himself, as he always did. 'This car can go into that corner of the new garage. And the two buses can go over here together. And the little lorry can stand next to the builder's van. And, let me see – where shall I put

the fire-engine? That ought to be near one of the entrances, in case it is called out suddenly.'

He played happily with his cars till lunch-time. Then he carefully carried his new garage indoors with all the cars and vans neatly arranged inside. Mother thought it looked really lovely.

'Don't go and fetch your old garage just now,' she said. 'Lunch is on the table. Go down afterwards, lock the shed, and bring the garage back then.'

So after dinner Harry went down the garden again. He carried his old garage out of the shed and set it down on the grass while he locked up the shed. He was just going to pick up his garage when he saw a robin standing on the handle of an old garden fork nearby. It sang a bright little song to him, and then flew even nearer, perching on a twig. Harry could almost have touched him!

'Are you hungry?' said Harry. 'Is that what you are saying? That you want a few crumbs? Well, follow me up

to my house, Robin, and I'll give you some. Come along!'

Harry returned to the house, followed by the robin. He forgot all about his old garage, left in the grass. The robin followed him closely, flying from bush to bush after him. Harry was delighted.

He fetched some crumbs and came out-of-doors again. The robin was still there. Harry scattered some crumbs round his feet, and the robin flew down at once. Once it even perched on Harry's foot, and he hardly dared to breathe in case he frightened it off!

It wasn't until he was going to bed that night that he remembered he had left his old garage down the garden in the grass. 'Bother!' he said. 'I'd better fetch it. If Dad finds it there tomorrow morning he'll be cross with me.'

So Harry put on his jacket and slipped out into the garden. It was quite dark now. He had to go slowly because he was afraid he would walk into the bushes. Ah – that big black shape must be the shed. Now – where was his garage? Why, oh why, hadn't he brought his torch!

He suddenly stopped. He had heard a peculiar sound – like a car hooting. But it must be a very tiny car because it was a very tiny hoot. It came from the ground nearby. Harry looked carefully all round.

He saw the lights of what must be a very small car indeed – and then another pair of lights. They were moving along, too. The cars, whoever they belonged to, were being driven carefully over the grass.

Harry went cautiously over and kneeled down. He was most amazed by what he saw! His old garage was there in the grass, where he had left it. But the door was open, there was a light inside – and two tiny cars were backing in, side by side!

'Hello!' said Harry, loudly and excitedly. 'Who's there? Who are you? And what are you doing in my garage?'

The cars stopped very suddenly indeed. A tiny head leaned sideways out of one of the drivers' seats. Harry could see it quite clearly.

'Hello!' said the head. 'Are you Harry?'

'Yes,' said Harry, astonished. 'But how did you know?'

'The robin told us,' said the head, nodding. 'He said you were kind, and gave him some crumbs when he was hungry. He said you wouldn't mind us having your old garage for our cars.'

Harry bent down even closer. He was so excited and astonished that he could hardly breathe. He saw that the head belonged to a little man with a beard. Another man very like him was in the other car. He poked his head out as well.

'But who *are* you?' said Harry. 'And why do you want my old garage?'

'I'm Bip Brownie, and he's Bop,' said Bip. 'We do a big business running round the rabbit-holes in our cars, taking odds and ends of carrots and things. But we haven't got a garage, and in this cold weather we're afraid that our cars will freeze up. Then we found this garage in the grass...'

'And the robin told us it was your old

The Boy Who Wanted a Pet

one, and you were kind and wouldn't mind us having it,' said Bop, suddenly joining in. 'But of course we'll not use it now. I expect you've come to fetch it, haven't you?'

'Well, yes, I have,' said Harry. 'But I've got a beautiful new one now, so I don't need this one. You can have it for your cars. I'd love you to! I'd love to think my old garage was having real little cars being driven in and out.'

'Thank you very much indeed,' said Bip, and he backed his car right in. Harry bent right down to look inside the garage, and saw that the two brownies had lit a tiny candle there. It really looked very exciting inside his garage, with two cars parked there, their headlights still on.

'Listen,' said Harry, suddenly. 'I think I'd better come back early in the morning and carry the garage to a safer place. My dad might find it here. It's no good telling him or anyone that two brownies are using it – they just wouldn't believe me. I'll come and put it in a very safe place where no one will find it. Then you can use it as much as you like.'

'Oh, thank you!' said Bip, switching off his car lights. 'That would be grand. There's a little copse not far off where hazel trees grow thickly. That would be a fine place for our garage – it's near all the rabbit-holes, too.'

'Isn't he a kind boy!' said Bop, coming out of the garage and shutting the doors. 'The robin was quite right about him. Bip, we ought to do something in return, you know.'

'Yes, we ought,' said Bip. 'Anything you specially want, Harry? A magic

pencil? Or a story in a book that never ends? Or an ice cream that never finishes? Or…'

Harry laughed. 'Oh dear – don't tell me any more! There's only one thing I really want, and I'll never have it.'

'What's that?' asked Bip and Bop together.

'Well, I want a pet,' said Harry. 'But it would have to be a pet that wasn't noisy, or dirty, or a thief, or wanted a lot of looking after, or could be eaten.'

'Impossible!' said the brownies, together. 'Think of something else and tell us tomorrow morning!'

'All right,' said Harry. 'Well, good-night – I really must go. Your cars will be quite safe now!'

Next morning before breakfast Harry was down the garden again. Where was his garage? Ah, there it was, in the grass. The doors were shut. He kneeled down and looked in at the window. Yes – the two tiny cars were still there. Where were Bip and Bop? Perhaps he had better whistle. He didn't need to.

The robin had seen him and had already flown to tell Bip and Bop that Harry was there. They appeared the very next minute, running at top speed out of a nearby rabbit-hole.

'Hello!' they said. 'Good boy! You've remembered to come!'

'Of course,' said Harry, and carefully lifted up the garage. But the brownies made him put it down again.

'No, no,' they said. 'We'll get our cars out first, and drive in front of you

to the hazel copse so that you will know the way.'

So they got out their cars and drove in front of Harry, bumping over the grass, hooting at a little mouse who came to see what was happening. Harry followed them, carrying the garage.

Soon they came to the little thicket of hazel trees, and Harry carefully put the garage down where they told him. It was well hidden under a bush.

'Thank you,' said Bip. 'And now, listen! We've found you a pet!'

'One that isn't noisy, or dirty, will never be a thief, doesn't need taking care of, and can't be eaten!' said Bop.

'What is it?' said Harry, astonished.

'Look – there he is!' said Bip – and would you believe it, down from the hazel tree bounded a little squirrel! He leaped on to Harry's shoulder and chattered in his ear.

'He's been asleep half the winter,' said Bip. 'But there's a warm spell on now, so he's woken up to find the nuts he hid. But he can't find them. He's got such a bad memory, you know. So if you like to buy him some nuts, he'll be glad to be your pet – your friend, really.'

'Will he?' cried Harry, in delight. He stroked the thick fur of the pretty little squirrel, and felt his big, bushy tail. What a lovely, lovely pet!

'He'll frisk in and out of your window, and come when you call him,' said Bop. 'He'll just want a few nuts, that's all. He'll go on being wild, but he'll be your friend, and he'll come when you call him. His name is Frisky Whiskers.'

The squirrel pulled at Harry's ear with tiny little paws. It felt lovely!

'He's the nicest pet in the whole world!' said Harry, joyfully. 'Mum can't possibly mind him! Oh, thank you – he's a wonderful exchange for my old garage!'

Well, he was, wasn't he? Harry went off with Frisky on his shoulder, and bought him some nuts. Then he took him home for his mother to see. And she loved him too. 'The pretty, frisky, dainty little thing!' she said. 'But don't think he'll be your pet, Harry. He won't. He's a wild thing, really. I can't imagine why he's suddenly made friends with you.'

But he is Harry's pet – and his friend and companion, too. He even goes to school with him sometimes, but he's so

very, very good that Miss Brown, the teacher, lets him stay in the classroom. Harry's very lucky, isn't he?

The old garage is still in the hazel copse, but the brownies have repainted it, so it looks very smart. I know you won't take it if you see it – but do just kneel down and see if Bip and Bop's cars are parked inside!

3

Snicker the Brownie

There was once a mischievous brownie called Snicker. He was always playing tricks – and they were hardly ever nice tricks!

Once he filled Dame Snippy's sugar tin with salt, and she couldn't *think* why all her cakes tasted so nasty that week. You see, she put salt into them instead of sugar.

Another time Snicker put some treacle inside Mr Doodle's hat, and dear me, the time Mr Doodle had, trying to get his hat off his head when he met Mrs Trips out shopping! Yes – Snicker was a very mischievous brownie!

But one day he went too far. Just listen! He thought he would go out for a walk, and see what mischief he could find to do. So off he went, his hands in his pockets and his bright eyes darting everywhere.

Before long he came to Cuckoo Wood. He walked down a path that he didn't know very well, and came to a small cottage in the heart of the wood. Snicker wondered who lived there. He looked all round it – and there, lying on the wall, were two big black witch-cats, sleeping in the sun!

Snicker the Brownie

Now, witch-cats have very long black tails – and Snicker saw these tails and planned a very naughty trick. He would tie them together whilst the cats were asleep – and then what a shock they would get when they woke up!

So, very quietly, he tiptoed up to the sleeping cats. He took their long, long tails and he tied them carefully into a huge knot. The cats slept on peacefully.

But the old witch who lived in the cottage looked out of the window and saw what Snicker had done. She

banged at her window in rage – and the cats woke up! They leapt down from the wall in fright – and, of course, as their tails were tied together, they could not run away. One cat tried to go to the house, the other tried to run out of the gate – and neither of them could move an inch because their tails were tied together and held them tightly!

Snicker began to laugh – and then a most surprising thing happened! The cats' tails came off! Yes, they really did – and what is more, those tails wriggled away like snakes, out of the garden gate, past Snicker, and slid off into the wood.

'Meow! Meow!' cried the two cats, in dismay. 'We've lost our tails!'

The witch came running down the path. She was in a fine temper. Before Snicker could escape she took him by the shoulders and gave him a good shaking.

'You nasty, mischievous little brownie!' she cried. 'Now just you go after those tails and bring them back, or I'll turn you into a jumping frog! Do you hear?'

Snicker was frightened. He really hadn't meant the tails to come off. He had forgotten that the tails of witch-cats are very magic, and come off easily.

'I'm sorry,' he said to the witch. 'I'll go at once. Don't punish me. I'll go this very minute!'

'They leave a silvery trail behind them just like a snail does,' the witch told him. 'Bring those tails back tonight - or you'll find yourself a jumping frog!'

Snicker ran off. He saw the silvery trail the tails left and he followed it. Through the wood he went - and waded over a stream - and then across a buttercup field - and then up a very steep hill - and then down the other side - and then through a little village of toadstool houses. Dear, dear, what a long way those tails had gone!

At last the silvery trail came to an end. It stopped at the door of a small crooked cottage, painted a peculiar yellow. Snicker didn't like the look of it. He knew a goblin lived there – and goblins who live in yellow houses are usually bad tempered. Why had the tails gone there? Oh dear!

Snicker knocked at the door. A goblin opened it. He had brown wrinkles like tram-lines across his forehead, and no chin at all. Snicker didn't like the look of him.

'Please,' he said, 'I've come for the tails.'

'Tails!' said the goblin crossly. 'What tails?'

'The tails that came here,' said Snicker. 'Please give them to me, or I'll be turned into a jumping frog!'

'How did they come off?' asked the goblin.

'I tied them together, and when the cats ran away, the tails pulled and came off,' said Snicker, going very red.

'Ho!' said the goblin. 'Then the tails don't belong to *you*. I shall keep them!'

He slammed the door. Snicker stood outside wondering what to do. He knocked again. 'Go away!' roared the goblin. Snicker went round to the back door. It was open. He peeped inside. The goblin was busy untying the two tails from their knot.

'Tails, come to me!' shouted Snicker. The goblin looked up, frowned angrily, and held on tightly to the wriggling tails, which were trying their hardest to go to Snicker. But he could not hold them – and, in a rage, he flung them at Snicker, saying, 'Take them, then –

and much good may they do you!'

The tails wriggled and flapped – and Snicker didn't like them at all. He turned to run away – but those tails fastened themselves to the back of him as he ran – and there was Snicker with two long black tails!

He couldn't get them off! They were growing on him! Wasn't it dreadful? The more he tried to tug them off the more he hurt himself, and at last, with tears running down his cheeks, he

made his way back again to the witch's cottage.

'I've brought the tails back,' he told her. 'Here they are - growing on me. Please take them off.'

'Oh, I don't want them after all,' said the witch. She pointed indoors. 'Look! My cats have both got nice long tails again. A gnome came by today selling tails, so I bought two. You can keep your tails now!'

'But I don't WANT the tails!' cried Snicker in dismay. 'I don't! I don't! Everyone will laugh at me if I go about with two tails - especially ones like these that wave about so! Oh, do please take them off!'

'No,' said the witch. 'It's a good trick to play on you, Snicker! It will make people laugh and laugh.'

'How unkind of you!' said Snicker.

'Well, you are always playing tricks yourself, and laughing at others,' said the witch. 'Now you know what it feels like to be laughed at. I hope you enjoy it!'

She slammed the door and left poor Snicker outside. The brownie went home - and how everyone laughed at him and his two waving tails! It was dreadful!

Snicker wore them until he met a wizard who knew how to take them away. He had to pay the wizard a silver sixpence - but oh, how glad he was to see those two tails packed into a sack and taken away on the wizard's shoulder. The tips just showed out of the neck of the sack, waving about in the air.

'Well, that's the last of *them*!' said Snicker. 'And they've taught me a lesson! I shan't play unkind tricks on anyone again - only just nice funny ones! It's not nice to be laughed at unkindly.'

If ever you meet a brownie called Snicker say 'Tails!' to him! If he goes red you'll know it's the brownie in this story.

4

The Little Old Donkey

Neddy was an old grey donkey. He belonged to Farmer Meadows, and he had lived with him for many, many years. Each day he took the milk round for the farmer, and stopped at the doors whilst the farmer asked what milk was wanted, and poured it out from the big cans on Neddy's back.

But now Neddy was old. He did not like to drag the cart that the farmer's wife sometimes went to market in. He did not like to carry Toddy, the man who borrowed him when he wanted to ride to the next town.

The cart was heavy and so was Toddy. The milk-cans did not weigh so much, and Neddy liked taking those round with his master. But his back was old and tired now, and he was sometimes cross when he found that he was being put into the cart, and knew that he would have to drag it and the farmer's big wife, right to market and back again.

The farmer was angry with him. 'Come come, Neddy!' he said. 'Do as you are told! If you cannot do your work, I must sell you!'

'He is getting old,' said Tilly, the farmer's servant-maid. 'He is as old as I am!'

'He won't be much use soon,' said the farmer. 'I'd better sell him and get another donkey. Perhaps Toddy would buy him.'

Neddy was sad to hear this. He loved the farm he had lived in, and he loved his master, though the farmer was sometimes impatient and cross. He did not want to be sold to Toddy, who would ride him hard, and feed him badly. He drooped his grey head and felt unhappy.

Now one morning the farmer was ill.

He could not get out of bed, and he lay there and groaned and grumbled to his wife.

'I'll have to spend a few days in bed,' he said. 'I twisted my back the other day, and it will have to get right.'

'What about the milk-round?' asked his wife. 'We can't let our customers go without their milk. I can't take it myself and Tilly must do the cooking.'

'Well, the milk will have to be wasted then,' said the farmer. 'There's no one to take it – and if there were, there is no one who knows the round and who would know which person to call on.'

So, to Neddy's surprise, no one came to take him on the milk-round that morning. Tilly had strapped the big milk-cans on his back, for she hadn't known that the farmer was ill – and the little old donkey stood by the front door, waiting for him to come.

When he didn't come, the donkey knew that he must be ill. So Neddy trotted off by himself. Why shouldn't

he go on the round? Didn't he know every customer? They all loved Neddy, and wouldn't they be pleased to buy their milk from him, even though the farmer was not with him? Of course they would, thought the little old donkey.

He trudged into the town. First he went to Mrs White's house and stamped on the pavement outside. Mary White, the little girl, saw him and called out to her mother:

'Here's Neddy with the milk – all alone, Mother! Isn't he clever? How much, do you want?'

The mother came to the door with a jug.

'Hee-haw!' said Neddy, which meant, 'How much milk?' The woman laughed

54

and dipped her jug into the can. 'One litre,' she said, and put the money into the purse that Neddy always carried by the cans. Neddy went off again and came to the next customer's house. Nobody was there, and though the donkey stamped on the pavement, nobody came to the door. Neddy looked for the bit of rope that pulled the bell inside the house. He had often seen his master pull this. So he took it between his teeth and pulled – jingle-jangle went the bell inside the house, and Mr Brown came to the door. He *was* surprised to see Neddy all alone!

'Hee-haw!' said Neddy politely. Mr Brown dipped his jug in the can, paid over his money, and Neddy went on again. By this time a few children had gathered round him, for they all knew Neddy, and they guessed that he had come to sell his milk without his master.

'Clever old donkey!' they cried, patting him. 'Do you know your next customer, Neddy?'

Of course he did! He stopped at Mother Lucy's house and stamped hard. The old woman came out with her jug.

'Neddy's alone!' shouted the children. 'He's going round to all the customers by himself! He knows everyone!'

'I always said he was a clever beast,' said Mother Lucy, who was fond of the donkey. She took the milk she wanted, and put the money into the purse. Then she gave Neddy a fine red carrot. He said 'Hee-haw' again and moved off, chewing it. This was a good treat!

Well, Neddy went to every customer that his master served in the town, and by the time he had finished his round, he had no milk left and the purse was full! He had had another carrot and a half-turnip, so he had done well.

He trotted off with the empty milk-cans, still chewing a bit of turnip. He cantered in at the farm gate and went to the kitchen door. Tilly would be there he knew, and would unstrap the milk-cans.

Tilly and the farmer's wife had been wondering where the old donkey had got to. They had hunted everywhere for him. The farmer had been cross when he had been told that Neddy had disappeared.

'He'll trot about the fields with that milk in the cans and upset it all!' he said.

Tilly heard the donkey's hooves, and she ran to the door. When she saw the empty milk-cans and peeped into the purse and saw it bursting with money, she could hardly believe her eyes! She unstrapped the cans, gave Neddy a lump of sugar, and ran to the farmer and his wife with the cans and the purse.

'See what your faithful old donkey has done for you!' she cried. 'He has gone on the milk-round himself, and has sold the milk and brought back the money! Never did there live such a donkey as that one! He's worth his weight in gold!'

The farmer could hardly believe what Tilly told him. He emptied the money on to the bed and counted it. It was even more than usual!

'Wife!' he said, 'that donkey is a fine fellow. Old he may be, and not wishful to carry heavy weights – but he's a

faithful creature, and I'll not sell him to anyone!'

Tilly ran down and flung her arms round Neddy's neck. 'You're not going to be sold!' she said. 'You're the best donkey in the world, and the master knows it!'

'Hee-haw!' said Neddy. He was very happy. Each day he went on the milk-round by himself, and so famous did he become that his master had many more customers than usual!

He is still going his rounds, though he is very old now – but the farmer kept his word, and has never sold him. I hope he never will, don't you?

5

The Purple Pig

Jenny and William had to do an errand for their mother, and they didn't really want to go.

'I don't like old Mrs Lump,' said Jenny. 'She wears such big, thick glasses, Mummy, and one of her hands is all funny and knobbly.'

'Poor old Mrs Lump,' said Mother. 'She has such a bad hand, and she has to wear those thick glasses so that she can see. She is almost blind without them.'

'She looks so cross,' said William.

'She isn't really,' said his Mother. 'She is always worried about things, and she has had a hard life. Don't be afraid of a poor old woman. Go and take her this old coat of mine. I promised I would send her something to wear.'

The coat was packed up in a box. William carried it. They went down the lane to old Mrs Lump's tiny cottage.

They knocked at the door. There was no answer. Mrs Lump was at the bottom of her garden, hanging out some wet clothes, but the children didn't know that.

'Bother! She's out. Now we shall have to come back again,' said Jenny.

'No – let's open the door and pop the box on the table inside,' said William. 'Then we needn't even see her. I'm sure she is a cross old thing, whatever Mum says.'

The door was only on the latch, so William could easily open it. The children went inside the cosy little kitchen. A fire was burning there, there were flowers in a vase on the table, and a big cuckoo clock that ticked merrily.

'Look at that purple pig on the mantelpiece,' said William, and he pointed to a big china pig there. 'Isn't it ugly? How can Mrs Lump bear to look at such an ugly pig all day long?'

'It's a money-box pig,' said Jenny.

'It isn't,' said William.

'Well, look – here's the slit in the top where you put money – and underneath is the place you unlock to get it out,' said Jenny, taking the pig down from the mantelpiece.

Just then the cuckoo shot out of the clock and called 'Cuckoo' very loudly four times. Jenny got such a shock that she dropped the pig!

Crash! It fell in the hearth and broke into a hundred pieces. The children stared at it in dismay. Money rolled everywhere, all over the room.

'Quick!' said William, grabbing Jenny by the hand. 'Let's go before Mrs Lump comes back and sees what we've done. Quick!' And they ran out of the door and into the lane. They were frightened. How cross Mrs Lump would have been with them if she had come in and seen her broken pig!

'I expect she loved that purple pig and was very, very proud of it,' said William. 'I do hope she won't be too upset about it.'

'William,' said Jenny, suddenly stopping. 'William, we're running away because we're afraid of being scolded! And you know Mummy always says we must never run away from something we have done. You know she says that is being a coward. Are we being cowards?'

William thought for a moment. 'Well, yes, we are, I suppose, Jenny. But I don't want to be brave over this.'

'Nor do I,' said Jenny. 'But I shouldn't like myself a bit if I was a coward. I'm going back. You needn't come if you don't want to. I dropped the pig, not you.'

'Of course I'll come with you, Jenny,' said William, who was very fond of his sister. 'Oh dear – I hope Mrs Lump won't be too angry.'

They went back, and their knees shook a little when they knocked on the door. Mrs Lump opened it. 'Ah!' she said, peering at them through her thick glasses. 'Did you bring me this nice coat just now?'

'Yes, Mrs Lump,' said William, and then he began to stammer. 'And – and – and – I'm really very sorry – but, you see, we broke that money-box of yours!'

'The cuckoo cuckooed and made me jump,' said Jenny. 'And I dropped it. Did you love it very much? Can I buy you another one? I think I've got enough money.'

'Bless you, child, I was never more pleased in my life than when I saw that

66

ugly old pig broken!' said Mrs Lump, laughing. 'I've hated it for years – nasty, ugly, purple thing.'

The children were astonished. 'Well, why did you keep it, then?' William asked her.

'Ah, my sister-in-law gave it to me, and I used to put my money in it,' said

Mrs Lump. 'And then I lost the key so I couldn't get it out – and I didn't dare to break the pig because my sister-in-law would have been so hurt and cross. She's got a very bad temper, you know, and I didn't want to make her angry. So there the old pig stood, year in and year out, holding on to my money for all it was worth!'

'So now you're glad it's broken?' said Jenny, pleased.

'I should just think I am,' said the old woman. 'That was a good turn you did me. Could you pick up the money for me, do you think? My eyes are not very good now, and besides, I've some buns in the oven I must see to.'

The children picked up the money. There was a lot. Old Mrs Lump was very, very pleased.

'Why, I'm quite rich!' she said, 'and now I'll never have to sit and look at that ugly pig again!'

'Well, we'd better be going now,' said William.

'Going? Of course you're not!' said old

Mrs Lump. 'You're having tea with me. Oh yes, you are! I've got a pot of strawberry jam I want to open – and new chocolate buns hot out of the oven – and some ginger biscuits I've been keeping for a treat!'

So the children sat down to a glorious tea, and how they enjoyed it. Afterwards they helped old Mrs Lump to wash up because her poor hand was very bad that day.

'Kind little children you are!' said Mrs Lump, and her warm brown eyes looked at them through her thick glasses. 'Now just pop out and pick a bunch of daffodils to take home to your mother, and then I shall have ready two little presents for you, too.'

They picked the daffodils and went indoors again. Mrs Lump had some exciting presents for them. Jenny's was a box of big glass beads of all colours, which would be lovely to thread, and William had a little fox made out of wood. They were very pleased with them.

'Oh, thank you,' they said, and then Jenny said something else. 'You know, Mrs Lump, we ran away when we broke your pig – we weren't going to own up.'

'Ah – but you came back,' said Mrs Lump. 'It isn't the running away that matters – it's the coming back and owning up. I'm proud you did that. Most children I know wouldn't have come back – but you did.'

They said goodbye and went home.

'Oh, Jenny, I am glad we weren't cowards,' said William. 'I should have felt so ashamed.'

'And we wouldn't have known what a nice, kind, old lady Mrs Lump is, and we wouldn't have known how pleased she was to have the pig broken and give up the money it held,' said Jenny.

'We'll be friends with her now, and go and see her often,' said William. 'Jenny, Mummy's always right, isn't she? We must never run away from anything!'

6

The Great Big Fish

Ellen and Donald ran to the pier.
Mother had given them tenpence each
to go on. It would be fun to run right
out to the end and see the deep green
sea there.

'We might see a big fish too,' said
Ellen. 'Oh, I do wish we had a fishing-
rod like all the fishermen on the pier
have, Donald. I would so like to fish
and catch a great big enormous fish!'

'I believe these fishermen are going
in for a fishing match,' said Donald, as
the two ran along the pier. 'There are
so many of them today!'

It was quite true. The fishermen were
fishing that day for a prize - five
pounds was offered to the man who
caught the biggest fish.

The children looked in the baskets of all the fishermen as they passed. No one had caught a fish yet.

Suddenly they came to old Mr Brown. He lived next door to them and was the kindest old man you can imgine. He often gave them money and sweets, and once he had brought them a fine Easter egg full of tiny chocolate eggs and two yellow fluffy chicks.

'Have you caught a fish yet?' asked Ellen, stopping to talk to him.

73

The Great Big Fish

'Not yet,' said old Mr Brown. 'I haven't had much luck lately. I think all the fish must know my line too well!'

The children had a grand time on the pier. They looked at all the funny machines there and wished they had money to put in them. They watched the fishermen as they saw one after another pull up some fine fish. Old Mr Brown caught one too, but it was very tiny.

Then he pulled excitedly at his line and cried, 'I've got a big one this time!'

His rod bent till it almost broke – and then the line reeled up – and what do you suppose he had caught? A big old boot that had once belonged to a fisherman! How everyone laughed.

Mr Brown was disappointed. So were the children. The old man cut away the boot, and it fell back into the sea with a splash. Then he put fresh bait on his hook, and threw the line out again.

He waited and waited and waited. The children had their lunch with

them, so they sat down by him and waited too. But although the other fishermen caught many fish, old Mr Brown couldn't seem to catch any more at all.

'I'm quite stiff with sitting here so long,' he said at last. 'I think I'll go for a trot round the pier and back again, children. Do you mind staying by my rod whilst I go?'

'May I hold it for you, do you think?' asked Donald eagerly. 'I've never held a rod in my life. I'll be very careful.'

So kind old Mr Brown let him hold the rod. Then off went the old man trotting round the pier to stretch his legs. Ellen stood by Donald and watched the water into which the line disappeared.

And then suddenly a most surprising and exciting thing happened! The rod Donald was holding almost flew out of his hands! It was a good thing he had such a tight hold of it!

'It's a fish, a fish!' yelled Donald. 'Mr Brown, where are you, where are you?'

But Mr Brown was right down at the end of the pier. Ellen caught hold of the rod too. 'Wind this little wheel like Mr Brown does!' she said to Donald. So he wound in the line, and the fish on the end tried its best not to come with the line. It pulled and jerked – but Donald held it fast.

Another fisherman came to help, but Donald said he could manage. Ellen leaned over the pier-railings and squealed in excitement. 'I can see the fish, I can see it! It's a most enormous big one! Ooooh!'

Mr Brown appeared again, and as soon as he saw what was happening he rushed to Donald. He took his rod and began to play the fish – letting the line run out when the fish pulled very hard and reeling it in when he had a chance.

At last he had the fish. Another man had to catch it in a net as it came on to the pier, for it was so big.

The children were so excited that they could not stand still but jumped up and down all the time.

'Mr Brown, Mr Brown, your fish is the very biggest!' they shouted. 'Oh, how much do you think it weighs?'

It was weighed on the scales, and it was eleven pounds. Mr Brown was so

pleased. No one had caught such a big fish so far. Perhaps someone would catch a bigger one before the day was out. He would have to wait and see.

The children waited too. Every time a fisherman caught a fish they rushed to see how big it was – but no one caught such a big one as old Mr Brown.

At five o'clock, when the match ended, Mr Brown was given the prize of five pounds. He was so pleased that he simply couldn't stop smiling.

'You've had no tea,' he said to the children. 'You've been two big bits of luck for me, haven't you? Come along, and we'll go home and show this fine fish to everyone – then we'll go and have a nice tea together in a tea-shop.

We'll have shrimp sandwiches, chocolate cream buns, and two ice-creams each!'

So off they all went, and how everyone stared in surprise at the great big fish they carried! Mother said of course they could go to tea with Mr Brown, so they set off together to the tea-shop. They all ate a most enormous tea, and Donald and Ellen thanked Mr Brown very much and said they had never had such a lovely day in all their lives.

'Oh, it isn't finished yet!' said Mr Brown, beaming all over his red shining face. 'You've got to have a bit of my prize you know, for you helped to catch the big fish! Now, what do you think you'd like, Ellen? A big doll? And you, Donald? A box of soldiers?'

'I'd like a little fishing-rod, please,' said Donald, 'and Ellen would like one too. We would so like to go fishing ourselves!'

'Right!' said Mr Brown. So he bought them both a fine fishing-rod each, and then they went home to bed, carrying their new rods very proudly indeed.

Tomorrow they are going fishing on the pier. I wish I could be there, too, to see the very first fish they catch, don't you?

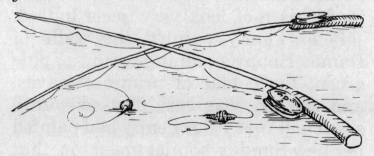

7

Hallo, Sooty Face!

Peter Penny was a house-painter. He was a mischievous little pixie, always ready with a cheeky answer, and always whistling the latest pixie song. He was a clever house-painter, so people put up with him.

That spring he was very, very busy. He painted the doors and windows of Brownie Longbeard's house a beautiful blue. Longbeard was very pleased – until he found that Peter Penny had painted his chimneys blue too, which made his roof look very queer indeed.

Peter Penny painted the walls of Dame Hoppy's dining-room a pale green, the colour of primrose leaves, and she too, was very pleased – until she found that Peter Penny had painted her new Sunday bonnet green too, that

she had left on the dining-room table one day.

Peter Penny also painted the gates that led to Wizard Heigho's castle. He painted them red and yellow in stripes and they looked very grand; but Heigho *was* cross when he found that Peter Penny had also painted his pony red and yellow as well. But Peter had gone off to the next town by that time, his money in his pocket, and his cheeky mouth pursed up whistling, 'A fairy loved a pixie who was very bright and tricksy,' the latest song in Fairyland just then.

'Any work to do here?' he asked the people he met. 'I'm Peter Penny the painter. I'm clever at painting walls, windows, doors, gates – anything you like.'

'Well, it's getting late in the year for painting now,' said the villagers. 'It's July you know; most people have finished their cleaning and their painting.'

'You might try at old Witch Sharp-eye's,' said a gnome. 'She was saying the other day that she really must get her house done again, for she was away all spring and didn't have anything done to it.'

'I'll try there,' said Peter Penny, and he skipped off to Witch Sharpeye's house. It stood on a hill, and was certainly in need of a coat of paint.

Peter Penny knocked at the door – rat-a-tat-tat, rat-a-tat-tat, rat-a-tat-*tat*!

'Stop that noise!' called a cross voice. 'One knock is enough.'

'Any house-painting needed, Mam!' called Peter Penny, sticking his cheeky head in at the door.

'Not if you knock like that,' said Witch Sharpeye, who was sitting in a rocking-chair, knitting at a long, long stocking. Round her sat twelve black cats, all watching her very solemnly.

'Your walls need a coat of paint,' said Peter Penny. 'Let me give them a coat of pale pink wash, and pick out your windows and doors in a soft blue, to match the blue and pink hydrangeas that are growing so beautifully in your garden, Madam.'

'That's a good idea,' said the witch, knitting away. 'How much do you charge?'

Hallo, Sooty Face!

'A piece of gold to you, Mam,' said Peter.

'Cheap enough, if you do your work well,' said the witch. 'Begin tomorrow – but a word in your ear, Peter Penny. Be polite to my cats, or I'll know the reason why!'

'MIAOW!' said all the cats together. Peter Penny bowed to them. 'The same to you!' he said.

The next day he began his work. He matched his paint with the lovely pink and blue hydrangeas and soon the dirty walls and windows began to look really beautiful.

Peter Penny would have been quite happy in his work if it hadn't been for the twelve cats. They all came to watch him at his job, and he didn't like it.

'Shoo!' he said. 'Shoo!'

But they wouldn't shoo. They just sat and watched him very solemnly, and if he did so much as a stroke of his brush wrong, they all spoke together in chorus.

'MIAOW! MIAOW!'

'Oh, go and chase your tails!' said Peter Penny, and flicked a spot of pink paint at the nearest cat. It caught it on the nose. The cat was offended and licked *off* the paint. It tasted so horrid that the cat hung its mouth open and looked disgusted. Peter Penny laughed.

But the cats would not go away. No, they sat round and watched Peter Penny at work, and if he sang or whistled too loudly, they all opened

their mouths and cried, 'MIAOW!
MIAOW!' till they drowned Peter
Penny's cheerful little voice and he had
to be quiet.

Peter Penny soon finished his work.
The witch's house looked very nice. She
paid him a piece of gold and told him to
clear up his things and take them away
as she was going out that morning,
and wanted him to be gone by the time
she came back.

Peter Penny watched her go down
the road to catch the bus. He grinned to
himself.

He mixed up a pot of pink paint and
a pot of blue paint. Then he went into
the kitchen and shut the door. The
twelve cats were there. Peter Penny
was very, very naughty. He painted
each cat's tail blue and each cat's head
pink. How strange and peculiar they
looked when he had finished!

'There!' said Peter Penny. 'That is for
watching me as if I were a mouse, all
the time I was painting. The witch will
get a shock when she comes in!'

But it was Peter Penny who got the shock – for the witch had missed the bus and had come back home again! Yes, really! She walked in at the door and stared in horror at her twelve black cats, all with pink heads and blue tails.

'So this is how you finish your jobs, is it!' she said to Peter Penny, who looked frightened. 'I've heard of your tricks before, Peter Penny. Now you will just come with me and get some soot to make my cats black again.'

'I d-d-d-don't know where any s-s-soot is,' stammered Peter Penny.

'Well *I* do!' said the witch. 'The goblin sweeps always store their soot in the middle of poppies. You can just take a bag and come with me. You will look into every poppy you see, and if there is black soot there, you will put it into your bag and bring it home for my cats.'

Poor Peter Penny! The witch gave him a sack, and took him by the collar. She marched him into the fields where

great red poppies grew, and every time he came to a poppy the witch stuck his head into it for him to see if there was any black soot there.

And as there always was, Peter Penny's face became blacker and blacker and blacker! He spluttered and choked, but it was no use – he had to look into the middle of every single poppy. Then he had to shake the soot into his bag.

By the time it was full Peter Penny's face was black all over. He did look dreadful!

The witch marched him back to her house and made him mix the soot with some magic water. Then he had to paint the cats' faces and tails black again. It took him a long time.

'Now go and wash your face in this water,' said the witch, handing him a bowl in which was some strange-looking water, silvery-grey. Peter Penny tried to wash his face in it: but alas for him there was magic in the silver water, and it made his face stay black so that he could not wash the soot off!

'You like to make things what they shouldn't be!' said Witch Sharpeye, 'and now you've got a taste of what it feels like. Your face shouldn't be black – but it is – and it will be for a long time! Ho, ho!'

Peter Penny went very red, but you couldn't see the red because his cheeks were black. He ran out of the house in a rage.

Nobody would let him paint their houses any more because he looked so dirty with his black face. So he had to turn himself into a sweep, and he always puts his soot into the poppies, just as the other sweeps do. You will find it there if you look. Don't forget.

And now nobody remembers that Peter Penny was once Peter Penny, a rosy-cheeked little pixie. They all call him Sooty Face! He won't answer, but it makes no difference.

'Hallo, Sooty Face!' everyone cries, as he goes down the road. 'Hallo, Sooty Face!'

Won't he be pleased when the spell works off and he can wash himself clean!

8

Mum's New Scissors

Mother came into the playroom looking rather cross.

'My scissors are no longer in my work-basket,' she said. 'One of you children must have borrowed them – and they are my new scissors, too. Who has taken them?'

'I haven't,' said Jean at once. 'I always ask you first.'

'What about you, Katie?' said her mother.

'Yes – oh dear, I did borrow them,' said Katie. 'I couldn't ask you because you were out. I took them yesterday.'

'Why didn't you put them back?' said Mummy. 'The least anyone can do when they borrow anything is to put it back! Where are they?'

'I don't know,' said Katie, trying to remember. 'Let me see – I took them out into the garden to cut flowers.'

95

'Well, you must have brought them back,' said mother. 'Where are they, Katie?'

'I'll go and look round the garden,' said Katie. 'I must have left them there.'

She ran out, ashamed, because she hadn't been careful with Mum's bright new scissors. Thank goodness it hadn't rained in the night, or they would be turning rusty.

She hunted everywhere for them, but she couldn't find them. She went back to tell her mother.

Mother frowned. 'You are always doing things like this, Katie. I can't have you growing up careless and forgetful. You will have to be punished. Those were my best new scissors – now I forbid you to play with your best new doll until you find my scissors.'

Katie didn't say anything, but she felt sad. She knew it was quite fair – but her best new doll was so lovely, and Katie took her out every single day for a walk.

'Now I shan't be able to,' she
thought. 'Poor Rosebud – she will
wonder why. And I mustn't even play
with her, either.'

Jean ran up to her. 'Katie – you can't
play with Rosebud, so may I? Do say I
can. You've only let me hold her once,
and I do love her. She's so pretty.'

'No, you can't,' said Katie, at once.
'She's my doll. I won't let you play with
her, if I can't.'

'All right,' said Jean, turning away.
'But I would be very, very careful – and
I'm sure Rosebud will be unhappy with
nobody at all to play with her and take

97

her out. You're not very kind.'

Katie looked at Rosebud, lying peacefully in her cot. Rosebud looked back, and Katie thought she seemed puzzled. Was she wondering why Katie didn't pick her up and love her as she usually did?

'It isn't your fault I can't take you out and play with you,' said Katie,

suddenly. 'I am unkind. Jean's right. Jean! JEAN! Come back.'

Jean came back. 'You can play with Rosebud and take her out into the garden for a walk,' said Katie. 'I *will* let you, Jean.'

'Oh thank you!' said Jean, pleased, and she ran to get Rosebud. She put on her pretty little rosebud hat, and her new coat. How sweet she looked!

Then she carried her out into the garden. It was very windy indeed. Jean had to smooth Rosebud's clothes down, because they kept blowing up. And then her hat blew off!

'Oh, bother!' said Jean. 'Katie wouldn't like that at all. Sit still on this seat, Rosebud dear, while I get your hat.'

She sat Rosebud down carefully. Then she looked round for the hat. Where was it? She hunted here and she hunted there. Where could that little rosebud hat have gone?

Then she suddenly saw it. It was perched on top of a big spray of

Michaelmas daisies and looked very strange indeed!

Jean ran to get it. The wind blew it off the daisies as she reached it, and it dropped down to the roots. Jean kneeled down and put her hand among the stems to get it. She lifted up the hat – and caught sight of something shining underneath.

'Why!' she cried, 'it's Mum's scissors! Katie! Quick, do come! See what I've found!'

She picked up the shining scissors and went to find Katie. She didn't run because her mother had said so often that it was dangerous to run with scissors – you might run into someone and hurt them with the scissor-points.

She found Katie and handed her the scissors. 'Your doll's hat blew off into the Michaelmas daisies' she said, 'and it dropped down to the ground and fell just on top of Mum's scissors. Here they are!'

'Oh!' said Katie, in delight. 'Thank you, Jean. Mum will be pleased. Now

I can play with Rosebud again.'

'Oh dear – so you can,' said Jean. 'I didn't have very long with her after all.'

'You shall have her as long as ever you like!' said Katie, and she hugged Jean. 'All the morning – and the afternoon, too, if you want to. How clever of Rosebud's hat to find the scissors for me!'

She gave Mother back her scissors and told her how Rosebud's hat had found them. Mother laughed.

'It was really you who helped them to be found, Katie,' she said. 'You had the choice of being kind or unkind to Jean – but you chose to be kind and let her play with Rosebud – and so she was able to find the scissors. That's the way things work in this world, you know!'

Her mother was right, of course. It's the way things work – but it was funny that Rosebud's hat had to find the scissors, wasn't it?

9

Granny's Lovely Necklace

Granny, Mummy, Daddy, Eileen and Jim were all down by the sea. It was such fun! The weather was fine and sunny, the sea was blue and the sands were smooth and yellow.

Granny was very happy. She did like being with everyone she loved. Eileen and Jim were very kind to her, because really she was the sweetest old lady you could imagine. She was always diving into her big bag for sweets, or cakes, or apples for Eileen and Jim, and she was always ready to listen to all they said or to tell them stories about the exciting things she did when she was a little girl.

Granny had a lovely necklace which she nearly always wore. It was made of shiny crystal beads with pretty blue ones here and there. Mummy and Daddy had given it to her for a birthday present, and Granny was very proud of it. Once she let Eileen wear it for a whole afternoon, and Eileen felt as grand as could be.

One day Granny lost her necklace. She simply couldn't *think* where it had gone. She felt for it round her neck – and it wasn't there!

'Oh dear, oh dear!' she said, in alarm. 'My necklace is lost! Eileen! Jim! Tell me, can you see my lovely necklace round my neck or anywhere on me at all?'

Eileen and Jim looked – but there was no shining necklace to be seen.

'Granny, it must have dropped off your neck when we went out in the boat this morning,' said Jim suddenly. 'You know, I thought I heard something fall into the water, and I thought it was my knife – but it must have been your necklace. I felt for my knife, and it was safely in my pocket.'

'Oh dear, do you really think it fell into the sea?' said poor Granny. 'Well, it's lost for good then. I shall never find it again. I am so sad about it.'

Granny looked so unhappy that Eileen and Jim felt unhappy too. They knew how horrid it was to lose anything they really liked. Once Jim had lost his favourite blue pencil and once Eileen had lost her second best doll – and they had both worried all day long.

Mummy and Daddy were told about the necklace. They were very sorry too.

'You had it on when you got into the boat this morning with the children,' said Mummy. 'I remember seeing it flash in the sun. Yes, Granny dear – you must have dropped it overboard when you leaned over to look at the fish or something.'

'Well, it's gone now,' said Granny. 'I must just put up with it.'

That afternoon Jim and Eileen were to go off for a picnic with Mummy, and they were going to leave Daddy to play golf and Granny to read by herself. But somehow the children didn't like going off to enjoy themselves when Granny was feeling rather upset.

'Let's put off the picnic till tomorrow,' said Jim to Eileen. 'I know what we'll do, Eileen – we'll get out our big shrimping net and we'll go shrimping to see if we can catch lots of shrimps for Granny's tea. You know how she loves shrimps. That will be a treat for her to make up for her lost necklace.'

'That's a good idea, Jim,'said Eileen. 'I'll fetch the net. I know where it is.'

Jim told Mummy about his idea. Mummy was pleased because she thought it was kind of the children. 'Granny won't be alone for tea if we don't go for a picnic,' she said. 'And *won't* she be pleased to have a feast of shrimps!'

Eileen and Jim went off with their net. The tide was coming in. 'It will bring the shrimps with it!' said Jim. 'I do hope there will be lots of big ones.'

They took off their shoes and stockings and ran to the edge of the water. They had seen the fisher-girls with their enormous nets shrimping at a certain place on the beach, and they guessed that was good for shrimps. They began to push the net lightly over the surface of the sand, a little way in the water.

'You can have a turn first, Eileen,' said Jim. 'I'll carry the basket.'

So Eileen had a turn first. The little waves curled round her legs. They were warm and tickly. Eileen liked to feel them. She pushed the net along, hoping there would be lots of shrimps in it when she looked.

'Have a look now,' said Jim. So Eileen lifted up the net carefully.

'Oooh! Oooh! Look at them jumping!' cried Jim in delight. 'You *have* caught a nice lot, Eileen! Let's put them into the basket.'

They put them into the basket. There were eleven! Six of them were so big that they really almost looked like prawns.

'Now your turn, Jim,' said Eileen. She gave him the shrimping net, and took the basket. Jim pushed the net along the sand eagerly. It was such fun to shrimp. He did hope he would catch as many shrimps as Eileen.

'I'll look and see how many I've got now,' he said at last. He lifted up the net – but will you believe it, there was only one tiny green crab in the net! Not a single shrimp jumped there! Jim was so disappointed.

'Have another turn, Jim,' said Eileen generously. But Jim shook his head.

'No,' he said, 'it's your turn, Eileen. I've had mine. I'll have another in a minute.'

So Eileen had a second turn – and do you know, when she lifted up the net again she had fourteen shrimps! They were nearly all big ones. She could hardly believe her eyes.

'I really am lucky,' she said to Jim, as they emptied the shrimps into the basket. 'Now your turn again, Jim.'

Poor old Jim! He didn't catch any

shrimps when he had his second turn either – and not even a crab – only a big piece of seaweed. He was dreadfully disappointed. He couldn't think why he was so unlucky.

'Perhaps you push the net too deeply into the sand and frighten away the shrimps before they get into the net,' said Eileen. 'I'll have my third turn now. I wonder if I'll catch any more!'

Eileen was certainly lucky that afternoon. She caught forty-three shrimps

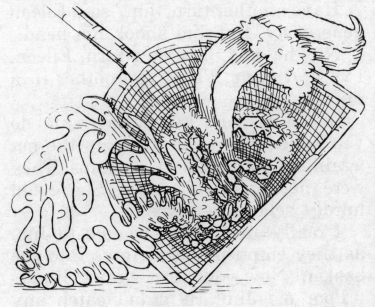

altogether, though poor Jim didn't catch one. But he caught something much better. Listen!

He was having his last turn. He lifted up the net to see if he had got a shrimp *this* time – and he saw something glittering in the net. Whatever do you think he had caught? Guess!

He had caught Granny's beautiful necklace! What do you think of that? The tide had brought it in to shore and it was lying half-buried in the sand at the edge of the waves. Jim had shrimped just there – and the necklace had slid into his net.

'Eileen! Eileen! Look, I've got Granny's necklace!' shouted Jim, in great excitement. 'Oh, do look!'

'Jim! Oh, how lovely! What a surprise! Whatever will Granny say!' cried Eileen in delight. 'Quick! Let's go and tell Mummy.'

So off they ran. Mummy was simply delighted. 'I know what we'll do,' she said. 'I'll cook the shrimps for tea and we'll put them into a covered dish – and we'll wash the necklace and put that into a covered dish, too – and we'll tell Granny that you've each caught her something for tea! Won't she be excited!'

So at tea-time there were two covered dishes on the table. 'I caught you what's in *that* one!'

Granny opened the first dish. It was full of delicious shrimps.

'Oh, how lovely!' she cried. 'What *can* be in the other dish?'

She took the cover off – and when she saw her lovely necklace glittering there, she could hardly believe her eyes!

'My necklace!' she said joyfully. 'Oh, my lovely necklace! Children, do please tell me how you found it.'

So they told her how they had given up their picnic to catch her some shrimps for tea – and how Eileen had caught her such a lot of shrimps – and Jim none – and then how he had caught the glittering necklace!

'You are two good, kind children,' said Granny, hugging them both. 'You have given me two beautiful surprises,

112

and now it is my turn to give *you* one! I shall buy Jim that steamer he wanted so much yesterday – and I shall buy Eileen a new spade because hers has a broken handle.'

'Oh Granny, Granny, it was a good thing after all that you lost your necklace!' cried the children. 'You have got a feast of shrimps – and we shall have new toys!'

'And I have seen how kind my two children can be,' said Mummy, smiling. 'So we are all happy.'

Granny had a new clasp put on her necklace, and she still has it. She told me this story to tell to you. I do hope you like it!

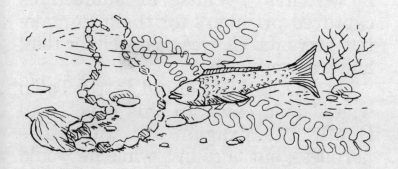

10

The Goblin and the Dragon

Once upon a time there was a green goblin called Crooky. He was just like his name, as crooked a goblin as ever lived in Little Town. He didn't tell the truth, he took things belonging to other people, and he was the worst tale-teller anyone could imagine.

No one liked him, no one smiled at him and no one asked him out to tea. Crooky hadn't a single friend, and didn't want one. He was only welcomed by witches, because he sometimes captured prisoners for them to make into servants. He was paid well for that, and was very rich.

Up on the hill behind Little Town was a deep cave. In this cave lived Goofle the dragon. He was quite harmless, but once in a while he would get terribly hungry; then all the pixies and brownies and goblins kept out of his way till he had fed on the cartful of bananas that the Lord High Chamberlain sent him as soon as he knew the dragon was hungry again. It was said that Goofle might forget his liking for bananas and eat a pixie, if one was near at that time.

Crooky often saw the dragon, because the goblin's house was near the cave. But Goofle didn't like Crooky at all, and wouldn't speak to him. He knew that he was a bad goblin and even dragons like to choose their friends.

This made Crooky very cross, and he was always trying to get Goofle to be friendly with him, so that he might be able to say, 'The dragon asked me to tea in his cave,' or 'The dragon had a picnic with me yesterday,' as the other little folk did. But Goofle turned his head away and sniffed loudly whenever Crooky came near, and wouldn't have anything to do with him at all.

Now one day Crooky went to a meeting to hear what arrangements were to be made to greet the King when he came on his yearly visit to Little Town. A pixie and an elf began to quarrel, and all the others tried to stop them.

'Be quiet, Flip!' cried the brownies near by. 'You look as ugly as the old dragon when you frown like that!'

'Don't lose your temper, Gobo!' cried the pixies to the elf. 'You will grow as ugly as the dragon if you do!'

Now as soon as Crooky heard them calling out these things, a plan came into his mind. Suppose he went to tell the dragon that the little folk called him ugly, surely Goofle would be pleased with him, and would be so angry with the other folk that he would go into the town and eat them all up. Then he and Goofle would be friends, and perhaps the dragon would make Crooky King of Little Town.

'Now, that's a good idea of mine,' said Crooky to himself, and he slipped out of the meeting-hall to think about it. 'I will pretend to be very much grieved to think that anyone should call Goofle ugly, and I will tell him he is beautiful, and that he should punish those who think he is not. He will be my friend after that, and everything will be lovely.'

So the very next day Crooky started out to the dragon's cave. Goofle was lying out in the sun, having a sun-bathe. He was not beautiful – indeed he really was very ugly, for he had scales all over his body, a long spiky tail, and when he breathed, smoke came out of his nose.

'Hello, Goofle,' said Crooky, in a very cheerful, friendly voice. The dragon took no notice of him, and pretended not to see or hear him.

'Hello, Goofle!' shouted Crooky. 'I say, I've got something to tell you. You will be surprised to hear it. It's something I've heard about you, and you won't be a bit pleased to hear what people say about you. As I feel very friendly towards you, I thought it was my duty to tell you.'

Goofle said nothing. He yawned very widely, and shut his eyes. Then, quite suddenly he felt terribly hungry. Once

every fifty days he felt like that, and it just happened to be the fiftieth day that morning. He wondered whether the Lord High Chamberlain was sending his cartful of bananas, and he opened his eyes to look down the hill to see if it was coming.

But it wasn't. The Lord High Chamberlain had made a mistake for once, and thought that it was only the forty-ninth day. The bananas were ordered for the next day instead.

Crooky the goblin didn't know that it was the fiftieth day. He went quite near to the dragon and spoke to him once more.

'Do listen, Goofle,' he said. 'I have something surprising to tell you. Do you know that everyone calls you ugly? What do you think of that?'

Goofle put his paw behind his ear, and pretended that he was hard of hearing, though he could quite well hear every word that the horrid little goblin was saying.

'Come nearer,' he said. 'I'm deaf in one ear and can't hear out of the other. Come nearer, Crooky!'

So Crooky came nearer.

'Sit on the end of my tail, Crooky,' said the dragon. 'I'm terribly deaf this morning. Sit on my tail.'

So the little tell-tale sat on the end of the dragon's spiky tail, and began to speak again.

'People down in Little Town say that you are very ugly,' he said. 'I think you ought to eat people that say unkind things about you. I think you are very beautiful.'

Goofle pretended he still couldn't hear.

'Sit on my back,' he said. 'There's a buzzing in one of my ears and a singing noise in the other. I can't hear what you say. Sit on my back, Crooky.'

So Crooky sat on the dragon's back, and began to shout. But Goofle only shook his head.

'One ear's deaf and the other's no good,' he said. 'Sit on my head, Crooky, sit on my head.'

So Crooky sat on the dragon's head, and began to shout again. But still it didn't seem to make the dragon hear.

'Sit on my big front tooth, Crooky,' he said. 'Sit on my big front tooth.'

So Crooky sat on the dragon's big front tooth – and then Goofle opened his mouth very wide indeed, jerked back his head, and shut his teeth with a snap.

Where was Crooky? He was gone!

The dragon smiled a wide smile, and felt that he could wait for his bananas now. In the distance he saw two or three brownies and he called to them.

'Ho there, brownies!' he cried. 'Come here a moment. Crooky said you call me ugly. I hope that that is true. You do think I'm ugly, don't you?'

'Of course we do,' said the brownies, in surprise. 'We have always told you so, Goofle. There isn't such a thing as a beautiful dragon, as you very well know. It is right for you to be ugly.'

'I thought so,' said Goofle with a pleased sigh. 'That stupid Crooky called me beautiful, and it made me feel so angry. I couldn't bear to be a beautiful dragon! Why, everyone would laugh at me!'

'Where is Crooky now?' asked the brownies, looking round. 'We will scold him for trying to tell tales. He is the horridest goblin that ever lived!'

The dragon went red, and hung his head.

'Well, you see,' he said. 'Crooky sat

on my big front tooth – and when I opened my mouth, he fell down my throat. I'm afraid you won't see him any more.'

'Good gracious!' cried the brownies in a fright. 'Why, it must be the fiftieth day! We must go and see about your bananas!'

Off they scurried and sent a message to the Lord High Chamberlain begging him to send the bananas at once. Then they went to tell the news about Crooky to everyone in Little Town.

Nobody said they were sorry, and nobody said they were glad – but Little Town was ever so much nicer without Crooky! As for Goofle the dragon, he ate up every one of his bananas, and then went to sleep very happy.

11

The Kind Little Dog

Once upon a time there was a little dog called Sandy. He belonged to a little girl. Her name was Susan, and she and Sandy loved one another very much.

Susan and Sandy were staying by the sea. Every day Susan dug in the

sand and Sandy dug too. He dug with his paws, and Susan dug with her spade. But Sandy managed to dig just as big holes as Susan.

One afternoon Susan lay down on the sand and fell fast asleep. It was hot and she was sleepy. Sandy wasn't sleepy at all. He wandered off by himself to sniff about over the beach. Perhaps someone had left a bag of old sandwiches about. Sandy thought he would like those!

He came up to an old man who was sitting reading a newspaper. If Sandy had stopped to look at the old man's face he would have seen what a cross, bad-tempered face it was. But Sandy didn't look at it. He had found something rather exciting.

The Kind Little Dog

In the sand by the old man's chair Sandy had smelt a nice smell. He began to dig to see what it was. It came from a cardboard box that had had a pork pie in it. The smell had been there. Sandy got very excited indeed.

He scraped at the sand and he scraped. He dug quite a big hole - and oh, my goodness, what do you think happened? He dug the hole rather near to one leg of the old man's deck-chair - and suddenly the chair tilted sideways and went into the hole. The old man nearly fell out - and he *was* cross! He glared round at Sandy and then he caught hold of him by his collar. He shook him well and hit him on the head. Sandy yelped and ran away. The man picked up some big stones and threw them after the little dog. Two hit

him. One hurt his hind leg and the other hit his head.

Poor little dog Sandy! He couldn't understand why anyone should be so unkind to him. He ran to Susan, who had wakened up and was very cross and upset to see her little dog so unkindly treated. She hugged him and looked at his leg and his head where the stones had hit him.

She took him home and bathed his leg, because it was bleeding. Sandy did like being petted and fussed. It was very nice.

The next day Susan and Sandy went down once more on the beach. It was such a windy day. The hair on Sandy's back blew up in the wind and the hair on Susan's head blew up too.

Susan looked to see if the cross old man was there. He was. He sat in his chair reading his paper, his straw hat on his head. And suddenly, as Susan looked at him, the wind came along and whipped that straw hat right off the old man's head. Wheeoo!

The hat rolled over the sand. It went as fast as a ball, for the wind was having a lovely game with it. Susan wondered if she should run after it – then she remembered how unkind the man had been to her little dog, and she didn't move a step. But Sandy did! He tore after that hat, barking to it to come back!

But the hat went on and on – and the wind laughed to itself as it blew it farther and farther away! Wheeeoo! Wheeeee! Wheeeeoo!

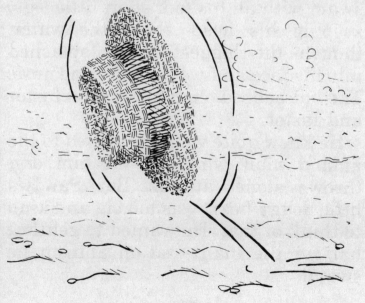

And then, just as Sandy was about to pounce on that hat, the wind blew it into the sea! It rolled right through the little waves till a big wave caught it and filled it with water. But the hat bobbed up again, floating on the sea merrily.

'Oh, my nice new hat!' groaned the old man. 'It's gone for good now!'

Sandy barked loudly. He splashed into the sea and raced through the little waves after the hat. But it was in deep water. Still, Sandy could swim! He swam with all his four short little legs, keeping his head above the water, though the biggest waves splashed into his face and wet his ears and nose. The hat bobbed on. Sandy swam faster and faster.

He knew quite well it belonged to the unkind man who had hit him and thrown stones at him. But, Sandy's little doggy heart was too big and kind to think of that. He wanted to get that hat for the man - so on and on he swam!

The Kind Little Dog

Susan called him. She was afraid he might drown in such deep water. 'Come back, Sandy, come back!' she cried. But the wind and the sea made such a noise that Sandy couldn't hear her. He saw the hat quite near. He swam hard with all four legs. He reached the hat at last - and snapped at it with his white teeth. He had it, he had it! Clever little dog, Sandy!

He turned and swam back to the shore, tired and panting. He held the hat firmly in his mouth. He came to the sands at last and shook himself. He ran to the old man and laid the hat down at his feet, his tail wagging away fast.

'Thank you, little dog,' said the old man, picking up his hat. He beckoned to Susan. She came running over.

'Your dog has done me a good turn,' said the man. 'Would you like a nice new tenpenny piece? I have one in my pocket?'

'No, thank you,' said Susan.

'Well, what would you like?' asked the man. 'Tell me, and I will do it for you?'

'Do you know what I would like?' said Susan, looking up at the old man. 'I would just like you to promise me something, please. You hurt my little dog yesterday, and I was sad. Will you please promise me not to hurt any dogs again? That would be better than tenpence. You were unkind to my little dog, but he wasn't unkind to you. He did his best to help you.'

The old man stared at Susan. 'Well, well, well,' he said at last. 'It's the first time I've been told that a dog can behave better than I can. But I do believe you are right. I'll give you my promise, little girl. I will never be unkind to dogs again.'

He patted Sandy, and Sandy wagged his tail hard again. Then the old man, quite forgetting that his hat was wet, put it on his head and walked off. Susan watched him go. Then she hugged Sandy.

'You are a good, kind little dog, and I love you!' she said. 'I don't expect that old man will ever hurt a dog again.'

And, do you know, he didn't! Sandy had taught him a lesson, hadn't he?

12

Tale of a Teddy and a Mouse

The new teddy bear was very small indeed. The toys stared at him when he first came into the playroom, wondering what he was.

'Good gracious, I believe you're a teddy bear!' said Amelia Jane, the naughty doll. 'I thought you were a peculiar-shaped mouse.'

'Well, I'm not,' said the small bear sharply, and he pressed himself in the middle. 'Grrrrrr! Hear my growl? Well, no mouse can growl, it can only squeak.'

'Yes. You're a bear all right,' said the pink rabbit. 'I hear you've come to live with us. Well, I'll show you your place in the toy cupboard, right at the back.'

'I don't like being at the back, it's

too dark,' said the little bear. 'I'll be at the front here, by this big brick-box.'

'Oh, no, you won't. That's *my* place when I want to sit in the toy cupboard,' said Amelia Jane. 'And let me tell you this, small bear, if you live with us, you'll have to take on lots of little bits of work. We all do. You'll have to wind up the clockwork clown when he runs down, you'll have to clean the doll's-house windows, and you'll have to help the engine-driver polish his big red train.'

'Dear me, I don't think I want to do any of those things,' said the bear. 'I'm lazy. I don't like working.'

'Well, you'll just have to,' said Amelia Jane. 'Otherwise you won't get any of the biscuit crumbs that the children drop on the floor, you won't get any of the sweets in the toy sweet-shop – and we're allowed some every week – and you won't come to any parties.'

'Pooh!' said the bear, and stalked off to pick up some beads out of the bead-box and thread himself a necklace.

'He's vain as well as lazy,' said the rabbit in disgust. 'Hey, bear, what's your name? Or are you too lazy to have one?'

'My name is Sidney Gordon Eustace,' said the bear, haughtily. 'And I don't like being called Sid.'

'Sid!' yelled all the toys at once, and the bear looked furious. He turned his head away and went on threading the beads.

'Sidney Gordon Eustace!' said the clown, with a laugh. 'I guess he gave himself those names. No sensible child would ever call a teddy bear that. Huh!'

The bear was not much use in the playroom. He just would not do any of the jobs there at all. He went surprisingly deaf when anyone called to him to come and clean or polish or sweep. He would pretend to be asleep, or just walk about humming a little tune as if nobody was calling his name at all. It was most annoying.

'Sidney! Come and shake the mats for the doll's-house dolls!' the pink

rabbit called. No answer from Sidney at all.

'Sidney, come here! You're not as deaf as all that.' The bear never even turned his head.

'Hey, Sidney Gordon Eustace, come and do your jobs,' yelled the rabbit.

No answer.

'All right!' shouted the rabbit, angrily. 'You shan't have that nice big crumb of chocolate biscuit we found under the table this morning.'

It was always the same whenever there was a job to be done. 'Sidney, come here!'

But Sidney never came. He never did one single thing for any of the toys.

'What are we going to do about him?' said the big teddy bear. 'I'd like to spank him – but he's too quick for me. Amelia Jane, can't you think of a good idea?'

'Oh, yes,' said Amelia Jane at once. 'I know what we'll do. We'll get Sidney the mouse to come and do the things that Sidney the bear should do – and he shall have all the crumbs and titbits that the bear should have. He won't like that – a common little house-mouse getting all his treats!'

'Dear me, is the house-mouse's name Sidney, too?' asked the rabbit in surprise. 'I never knew that before. When we want him we usually go to his hole and shout 'Mouse', and he comes.'

'Well, I'll go and shout 'Sidney',' said Amelia Jane, 'and you'll see – he'll come!' So she went to the little hole at the bottom of the wall near the bookcase and shouted down it. 'Sidney! Sid-Sid-Sidney! We want you.'

The little bear, of course, didn't turn round – he wasn't going to come when his name was called. But someone very small came scampering up the passage to the entrance of the hole.

It was the tiny brown house-mouse, with bright black eyes and twitching whiskers.

'Ah, Sidney,' said Amelia Jane. 'Will you just come and shake the mats in

the doll's-house, please? They are very dusty. We'll give you a big chocolate biscuit crumb and a drink of lemonade out of the little teapot if you will.'

'Can I drink out of the spout?' said the tiny mouse, pleased. 'I like drinking out of the spout.'

'Yes, of course,' said Amelia Jane.

The little mouse set about shaking the mats vigorously, and the job was soon done.

'Isn't Sidney wonderful?' said Amelia in a loud voice to the others. 'Sidney the mouse, I mean, of course, not silly Sidney the bear. He wouldn't have the strength to shake mats like that, poor thing. Sidney, here's your chocolate biscuit crumb and there's the teapot full of lemonade.'

Sidney the bear didn't like this at all. Fancy making a fuss of a silly little mouse, and giving him treats like that. He would very much have liked the crumb and the lemonade himself.

He pressed himself in the middle and growled furiously when the mouse had gone.

'Don't have that mouse here again,' he said. 'I don't like hearing somebody else being called Sidney. Anyway, I don't believe his name *is* Sidney. It's not a name for a mouse.'

'Well, for all you know, his name

might be Sidney Gordon Eustace, just like yours,' said Amelia Jane at once.

'Pooh! Whoever heard of a mouse having a grand name like that?' said the bear.

'Well, next time you won't do a job, we'll call all three names down the hole,' said Amelia, 'and see if the little mouse will answer to them!'

Next night there was going to be a party. Everyone had to help to get ready for it. Amelia Jane called to the little bear.

'Sidney, come and set the tables for the party. Sidney, do you hear me?'

Sidney did, but he pretended not to, of course. He wouldn't set party tables! So he went deaf again, and didn't even turn his head.

'Sidney Gordon Eustace, do as you're told or you won't come to the party,' bawled the big teddy bear in a rage.

The little bear didn't answer.

Amelia Jane gave a sudden grin. 'Never mind,' she said. 'We'll get Sidney Gordon Eustace, the little

mouse, to come and set the tables. He does them beautifully and never breaks a thing. He can come to the party afterwards. I'll call him.'

The little bear turned his head. 'He won't answer to *that* name, you know he won't!' he said scornfully. 'Call away! No mouse ever had a name as grand as mine.'

Amelia Jane went to the mouse-hole and called down it. 'Sidney Gordon Eustace, are you there?' she called. 'If you are at home, come up and help us. Sidney Gordon Eustace, are you there?'

And at once there came the pattering of tiny feet and, with a loud squeak, the little mouse peeped out of his hole, his whiskers quivering.

'Ah – you are at home,' said Amelia Jane. 'Well, dear little Sidney, will you set the tables for us? We're going to have a party!'

The mouse was delighted. He was soon at work, and in a short while the four tables were set with tiny tablecloths and china. Then he went to help the doll's-house dolls to cut sandwiches.

The little bear watched all this out of the corner of his eye. He was quite amazed that the mouse had come when he was called Sidney Gordon Eustace – goodness, fancy a common little mouse owning a name like that!

He was very cross when he saw that the mouse was going to the party. Amelia Jane found him a red ribbon to tie round his neck and one for his long

tail. He was given a place at the biggest table, and everyone made a fuss of him.

'Good little Sidney! You do work well! Whatever should we do without you? What will you have to eat?'

147

The mouse ate a lot. Much too much, the little bear thought. He didn't go to the party. He hadn't been asked and he didn't quite like to go because there was no chair for him and no plate. But, oh, all those nice things to eat! Why hadn't he been sensible and gone to set the tables?

'Goodnight, Sidney Gordon Eustace,' said Amelia Jane to the delighted mouse. 'We've loved having you.'

After this kind of thing had happened three or four times the bear got tired of it. He hated hearing people yell for 'Sidney, Sidney!' down the mouse-hole or hearing the mouse addressed as Sidney Gordon Eustace. It was really too bad. Also, the mouse was getting all the titbits and the treats. The bear didn't like that either.

So the next time that there was a job to be done, the bear decided to do it. He suddenly heard the rabbit say, 'Hello! The big red engine is very smeary. It wants a polish again. I'll go and call Sidney.'

The pink rabbit went to the mouse-hole and began to call down it. 'Sidney, Sidney, Sidney!'

But before the mouse could answer, Sidney the bear rushed up to the rabbit. 'Yes! Did you call me? What do you want me to do?'

'Dear me, you're not as deaf as usual,' said the rabbit, surprised. 'Well, go and polish the red engine, then. You can have a sweet out of the toy sweet-shop if you do it properly.'

Sidney did do it properly.

The pink rabbit came and looked at the engine and so did Amelia Jane.

'Very nice,' said Amelia Jane. 'Give him a big sweet, Rabbit.'

150

The bear was pleased. He had done the mouse out of a job. The toys had been pleased with him, and the sweet was delicious.

And after that, you should have seen Sidney the bear rush up whenever his name was called. 'Yes, yes – here I am. What do you want me to do?'

Very soon the little mouse was not called up the hole any more and Sidney the bear worked hard and was friendly and sensible. The toys began to like him, and Sidney liked them, too.

But one thing puzzled the rabbit and the big teddy bear, and they asked Amelia Jane about it.

'Amelia Jane – how did you know that the mouse's name was Sidney Gordon Eustace?'

'It isn't,' said Amelia Jane with a grin.

'But it must be,' said the rabbit. 'He always came when you called him by it.'

'I know – but he'd come if you called any name down his hole,' said Amelia

151

Jane. 'Go and call what name you like – he'll come! It's the calling he answers, not the name. He doesn't even know what names are.'

'Good gracious!' said the rabbit and the bear, and they went to the mouse-hole.

'William,' called the rabbit, and up came the mouse. He was given a crumb and went down again.

'Polly-Wolly-Doodle,' shouted the big

bear, and up came the mouse for another crumb.

'Boot-polish,' shouted the rabbit, and up came the mouse.

'Tomato soup,' cried the big bear.

It didn't matter what name was shouted down the hole, the mouse always came up. He came because he heard a loud shout, that was all.

Amelia Jane went into fits of laughter when the mouse came up at different calls. Penny stamp! Cough-drop! Sid-Sid-Sid! Dickory-Dock! Rub-a-dub-dub!

The mouse's nose appeared at the hole each time. How the toys laughed – all except Sidney the bear!

He didn't laugh. He felt very silly indeed. Oh dear, what a trick Amelia Jane had played on him. But suddenly he began to laugh, too. 'It's funny,' he cried. 'It's funny!'

13

The Big Dog

One day a very big dog came running into the gates of Green Hedges. He was an ugly dog and a fierce one, and Bobs the puppy didn't like the look of him at all. The dog ran to the porch and ate up the cat's dinner. He ran to the pigeon bowl and crunched up the pigeon seed. He then went to the pond for a drink and drank so much that Bobs was really afraid he would empty the pond.

For four days the big, ugly dog came, and none of the animals at Green Hedges dared to stop him. At last they held a meeting about it, and everybody said his say.

'He's a wicked dog and ought to be stopped,' said Bobs.

'He's a perfect nuisance, and we really must do something!' said Sandy.

'I would scratch him if I could get near him,' said Cosy.

'And I would nip his tail if he didn't wag it so fast,' said Pitapat.

'What you should do is get an old muzzle and strap it on his mouth,' said Bimbo the kitten, who always talked a great deal and very loudly, too. 'You should stop him from eating things, then he wouldn't get my dinner or the pigeon's either. You should...'

'You are full of good ideas, Bimbo,' said Bobs, politely. 'But you talk too much. Also, we are not deaf, though you seem to think we are.'

'Well, you are stupid, and I have to shout to get any good ideas into your

head,' Bimbo said rudely. 'I tell you, Bobs, my idea is best of all – muzzle the dog and he will do no more harm.'

'Very well,' said Bobs. 'We will carry out your idea. Sandy, fetch that old muzzle from the rubbish heap next door. Bimbo, as it's your idea, you shall muzzle the dog yourself. Look, here's the muzzle – and there's the big dog just coming in at the gate! Hurry up and go to him before he eats your dinner again!'

Everyone looked at Bimbo, and he began to swing his tail crossly. Whatever was he to do?

'Take the muzzle quickly,' said Bobs, grinning.

'Well, I will go and muzzle that big dog,' said Bimbo at last. 'I am a very brave kitten. You are all cowards, because you dare not muzzle him.' He took up the muzzle and started off towards the dog. Then he looked back and said, 'I can put the muzzle on by myself, but I am not big enough to hold the dog still while I strap it on. Will you come and hold the dog for me, Bobs?'

'Er – er – I've a little job to do for the Mistress!' said Bobs, and he rushed away.

'Will you come and hold the dog for me, Sandy?' asked Bimbo. But Sandy suddenly remembered that he had a bone to see to, and he was gone.

'Will you hold the dog for me?' Bimbo asked Cosy and Pitapat. But they shook their heads and said that they had promised to go and meet the milkman. So Bimbo was left all alone. He grinned to himself and dropped the muzzle into the pond.

'Well, I can't muzzle the dog if nobody will help me!' he shouted in his loudest voice – and then he ran for his life! The big dog had seen him and Bimbo was not going to stop and say good morning.

After that nobody mentioned big dogs again, and I'm not surprised. Are you?

14

Simon's Clean Handkerchief

'Mother,' said Simon one day, 'the teacher says I *must* take a clean handkerchief to school each day.'

'Good gracious me, I should think so,' said his mother. 'You know where your clean handkerchiefs are, don't you, Simon? Well, just see you take one each morning.'

So the next morning Simon started off with a nice clean handkerchief. He was so pleased to have it that he carried it in his hand. He meant to show it to his teacher as soon as he got to school.

But on the way Simon had to climb over a stile. He laid his handkerchief carefully down on the top, and climbed over. And will you believe it, he left his handkerchief on the stile. When he got to school the teacher said: 'Did you remember your handkerchief today, Simon?'

'Yes,' said Simon – but, dear me, it wasn't in his hands and it wasn't in his

pockets. 'I've left it on the stile,' said Simon. 'Bother!'

As he came home from school he looked for his handkerchief – and there it was on the ground, in rags! Daisy the cow had come along and seen it on the stile. She had given it a chew and then spat it out. It was no use at all as a handkerchief now!

That afternoon Simon took another handkerchief from his drawer. 'I will tie a knot in it to remind myself to hold on to it all the way to school,' he thought. So he tied a big knot in the corner. Then off he went.

He climbed over the stile safely, his handkerchief in his hand. He went on jogging along happily. Suddenly he saw a butterfly and he went after it. It settled on a flower. Simon put down his handkerchief, and crept up to the butterfly. He pounced – but the butterfly was gone, flying high into the air!

'Bother!' said Simon, and skipped off to school. He had left his clean handkerchief on the ground.

'Where is your handkerchief, Simon?' asked the teacher.

'Oh,' said Simon proudly, 'do you know Miss Brown, I tied a knot in it to remind me to bring it. Wasn't that clever of me!'

'Well, where is it?' asked Miss Brown.

Well, of course, Simon couldn't find it anywhere! He had left it behind on the grass.

Miss Brown was cross with him.

'You are a naughty little boy,' she said. 'Now just remember it tomorrow, please.'

So the next morning Simon took another handkerchief from his pile. He hadn't been able to find the one he had

164

left on the grass, because the wind had blown it away.

'Now I really and truly will remember to take my handkerchief this time!' said Simon. 'I will not let it leave my hand all the way to school.'

Just as he started off, his mother called him. 'Simon, dear! Post this letter for me on your way, will you?'

'Certainly, Mother!' said Simon. He took the letter and ran off. He wondered if he remembered his six times table, because he knew Miss Brown was going to hear it that morning. So he began to say his tables:

'Six times one are six,
Six times two are twelve.'

As he was saying his tables he came to the pillar-box, red and shining in the roadway. He ran up to it, saying his tables all the time, and was proud to think he knew the whole of six times. But do you know what he did? He posted his handkerchief instead of his mother's letter! Oh, Simple Simon, whatever is anyone to do with you!

'Well, Simon,' said his teacher, as he ran into school. 'I hope you've got your handkerchief today!'

'Yes, Miss Brown,' said Simon proudly. 'I kept it in my hand all the time – look!'

He handed her – his mother's letter! Miss Brown stared in surprise.

'But this is a letter, not a handkerchief, Simon,' she cried.

'Oh my, oh my!' groaned poor Simon, looking at it. 'I must have posted my handkerchief! Yes – that's what I did!'

'Simon, I shall be very cross with you soon,' said Miss Brown. 'Please do try and bring a clean handkerchief this afternoon. I will give you one more chance.'

So Simon once more took a clean handkerchief from his drawer that afternoon. He put it into his pocket. He thought it would be safer there than in his hand! Off he started to school. But on the way he fell down. His knee bled, and his hands were covered with mud. Poor Simon! He took out his hand-

kerchief and scrubbed his hands. He
wiped his knee. Then on he went again.
But it was not Simon's lucky day. He
brushed against some wet paint, and
his nice jersey was covered with blue!
Out came the handkerchief again, and
Simon wiped off the blue paint.

But he did arrive at school with his
handkerchief, and proudly he showed
it to Miss Brown.

'Simon! What a horrid, dirty smelly
rag!' she cried. 'Surely it is not a

handkerchief! Didn't I say you were to bring a *clean* handkerchief? Just see you do tomorrow morning, or I will be cross!'

Simon cried all the way home, and when he told his mother what had happened she was cross with him. And she was crosser still when she found that he had lost his hat that morning too!

'Simon, you are the silliest child I ever knew!' she cried. 'Now, look here – this is one of your father's handker-chiefs, for you have used all yours. As you have no hat and the sun is very hot I am going to knot each corner of the handkerchief and make a cap for you out of it. You will wear it to school, and, goodness me, surely you can't lose it if you've got it on your head.'

Simon was pleased to have a hand-kerchief cap. His father's handkerchief was big and red with white spots. He felt very grand going to school with such a fine red cap on.

But, bless us all, when he got to

school he had forgotten that he had the handkerchief on his head! When Miss Brown asked him to show her his clean handkerchief, Simon turned out his pockets. But there was no handkerchief there!

'Simon!' said Miss Brown, in an angry voice. 'Do you mean to tell me you've forgotten again!'

'No, Miss Brown,' said Simon. 'I did bring a handkerchief with me this time, I really did! But, oh dear, wherever is it?'

'Take off your cap and come indoors,' said Miss Brown, looking very cross.

Simon took off his red cap – and no sooner had he got it in his hands than he saw that it was his father's nice clean red handkerchief!

'Miss Brown, Miss Brown, here it is!' he cried. 'I was wearing it on my head – and it's quite clean. Look!'

'Well, if you aren't the silliest little boy!' said Miss Brown. 'You've only *just* saved yourself a telling-off. Now, in future Simon, ask your mother to *pin* a clean handkerchief to your jersey each day – then perhaps you will be able to bring it safely to school, and I shall see it!'

So that is what Simon does now – but today his mother was away, so Simon found the safety-pin to pin on his handkerchief – but, oh dear, he made a mistake, and pinned on to his jersey the baby's best white coat. Whatever will Miss Brown say?

15

Don't Tell Anyone

George had a new suit and a new pair of boots. His mother had just bought the suit, and it fitted George beautifully. It was dark blue, and had a waistcoat like his father's. George was very proud of it.

'When can I wear it?' he asked his mother.

'Tomorrow,' she said. 'Auntie Winnie is coming to tea and you must be clean and tidy then.'

So after dinner the next day George put on his new suit. He tied his tie neatly, and brushed his hair till it shone. He put on his new boots and tied the laces tightly. My, he did look grand!

'Mother, could I have my watch to wear today for a treat?' he asked.

Don't Tell Anyone

He had a fine silver watch and chain that Uncle Dick had given him last Christmas. It was such a nice one that George hardly ever wore it for fear of losing it. But he did think it would be fine to wear with his grand new suit.

'Yes, you can wear it,' said Mother. So George took it out of its leather case and slipped the watch into his pocket, and slid the chain through a button-hole to the pocket on the opposite side. Now he really felt as grand as could be!

'Can I go for a little walk?' he asked his mother. 'I won't dirty myself.'

'Very well,' said Mother. 'Just go down to the sea and back.'

George lived by the sea, and he never got tired of watching the big waves in winter-time, and the people that came to bathe and paddle in the summer-time. He set off down the road and soon came to the front, where many people walked up and down, enjoying the hot sunshine.

George walked along the front slowly. He hoped everyone was noticing how

fine he looked with his silver watch chain across the front. Dear me, it wasn't often he looked so grand! Usually he was a very dirty, untidy little boy – but just for once he was quite different!

The tide was in and was splashing right against the wall. Some children were standing watching it, and with them was a small three-year-old girl. As George passed, the little girl suddenly slipped and fell splash into the sea below!

'Oh! Oh!' shrieked the other children. 'Mollie's in the sea! Oh, quick, Mollie's in the sea!'

George ran to the place where the little girl had fallen in. There she was, struggling in the deep sea below. Oh dear, would nobody come! There seemed to be nobody grown-up at all to come and save the little girl.

George could swim. He was the best swimmer in his class at school. He forgot about his best clothes, and before anyone knew what he was doing he had jumped straight into the waves below! He fell close by the choking little girl, and he caught hold of her. He began to swim with her to the steps. It was difficult because she would cling to

him so. But at last he got her safely to the steps and dragged her up.

The other children pulled her in, crying with fright. One of them saw how wet George was.

'How will you get dry?' she said.

'Don't tell anyone!' said George, shaking himself like a dog, and trying to squeeze the water out of his coat. 'This is my new suit and my mother would be so upset to see it wet. Don't tell anyone, will you! I'll try and dry it.'

By this time a crowd had collected and the little girl ws being dried and comforted. George was able to slip away. A man tried to stop him, but George wriggled off.

'Please don't tell anyone!' he begged. Then off he ran home. He crept in at the back gate. No one was about. Mother must have gone to meet Auntie Winnie. Good!

The little girl next door looked over the fence. 'Ooooh!' she said. 'How did you get wet like that? Won't your mother be cross?'

'Now *please* don't tell anyone!' said George. 'I want to try and dry my clothes before my mother comes home.'

He slipped indoors and ran up to his room. He took off all his wet things and squeezed the water out of them. And then he discovered something that made him stand still in horror. He had lost his lovely silver watch and chain!

'It must have fallen out of my pocket when I was swimming with that little girl to the steps,' said George. 'Oh, what a dreadful thing! I was so proud of that watch.'

The little boy was very unhappy about his lost watch and chain, but he had no time to stop and grieve about it. He really must dry his clothes before his mother came home!

He put on his dressing-gown and hurried down to the kitchen. He put all his clothes through the dryer to begin with, and then he stood the clothes-horse in front of the fire and spread out his clothes there. How long would it take them to dry? Oh, he did hope they

would be ready in time!

Mother had gone to meet Auntie Winnie at the railway station, and, as it was such a lovely afternoon they went down to the front for a walk. There they heard everyone talking about a brave boy who had jumped into the sea and saved a little girl from drowning. But nobody seemed to know who it was! The children who had been with the little girl knew who it was, but they said nothing, because George had begged them not to tell anyone.

Mother stayed with Auntie Winnie on the front by the sea until tea-time.

Then they made their way home.

And what was George doing? Well, his clothes were nearly dry, and he had put them on. They looked very queer – most crumpled and untidy – and his boots wouldn't dry at all, so he had had to put his old ones on. He didn't look at all nice, but it was the best he could do. He hoped Mother wouldn't notice.

Auntie Winnie was pleased to see him. Mother took one look at him and then turned away, vexed. How *could* George get his nice new suit all untidy and crumpled like that? It was too bad of him. George saw how vexed she looked, and he was unhappy. But Mother didn't scold him in front of Auntie Winnie.

'Show Auntie Winnie your silver watch and chain whilst I make the tea,' she said.

Poor George! He went very red, and didn't know what to say.

'I lost it this afternoon I'm afraid,' he said to Auntie Winnie.

Auntie Winnie wondered what was

the matter with George. He looked so hot and untidy and unhappy. Perhaps he wasn't well. She began to talk about her walk along the front that afternoon.

'And do you know, George,' she said, 'everyone was talking about a brave boy who had jumped into the sea and saved a little girl from drowning this afternoon!'

'Oh,' said George, going redder than ever.

'Wasn't it brave of him?' said Auntie Winnie. 'The little girl's mother does so want to know who the little boy was, so that she could thank him, but no one seems to know. He ran off without even giving his name. I wonder why!'

'Oh,' said George, going redder than ever. This was dreadful.

Mother had been listening, and watching George. She quickly went to him and felt his coat. It was damp.

'George,' she said. 'Was it *you* who jumped into the water after that little girl?'

'Yes, Mother,' said George. 'But I quite forgot I had my new suit on when I did it. I just couldn't help it. And I've lost my watch and chain. I'm so unhappy about that. But, you see, there wasn't anyone else nearby who could swim, so I just had to jump in. I have tried to dry my clothes, but they wouldn't dry properly.'

'Oh, George!' said his mother, and to George's surprise she suddenly hugged him as if she would choke him.

'What do you suppose a new suit matters, or even a watch and chain, so long as you are brave? You have saved that little girl from drowning, and I don't mind about your suit a bit.'

George was surprised and pleased. His mother made him change his damp suit and put on his jersey and shorts. He felt much more comfortable. Auntie Winnie was so nice to him too. He began to feel much happier.

And to George's surprise he soon found that he was quite a hero. Somebody said that it was he who had jumped in to save the little girl, and people told him he was a fine brave boy. Nobody scolded him for spoiling his new suit or for losing his watch!

And what do you suppose the little girl's mother gave George the very next day? She sent him a *gold* watch to wear, with a strong leather chain so that it couldn't possibly be lost. He was so very proud.

'You deserve it, George,' said his mother. And his father said so too.

'Well,' said George, 'I tried not to let anyone know, because of my new suit – but it seems as if everyone knows my secret now. And I don't mind a bit, because you are all so nice to me.'

I've seen George's watch. It really is a fine one, I can tell you.

16

The Bad Cockyolly Bird

The Cockyolly bird lived in the nursery with the other toys. He was a colourful creature, with red plush wings, a yellow tail, and a green body. He could be wound up, and then he walked along in a jerky manner, saying 'Kack, kack, kack!' as he went.

Now the Cockyolly bird was a great nuisance. He was always picking up things that belonged to other people, and running off with them.

He ran off with the big doll's hairribbon, and she couldn't find it anywhere. Where do you suppose he had put it? He had stuffed it up the tap in the basin. When Nurse turned on the tap, out came the ribbon! She was so surprised.

He ran off with the baby doll's shoes. The baby doll had taken them off because they were rather tight, and she was enjoying herself, running about in her bare feet. And when she wanted her shoes they had gone.

'The Cockyolly bird took them,' said the clockwork mouse. 'I saw him. He has thrown them out of the window!'

So the baby doll had to climb down

the apple tree outside and go to hunt for her slippers in the dark. She didn't like it at all.

Everyone scolded the Cockyolly bird, but he only grinned and said 'Kack! If I could find some place to put your things so that you wouldn't find them so easily, I'd hide them away properly.'

And then one day the Cockyolly bird *did* find a place to put things – where do you suppose it was? You'll never guess! It was in the big money-box that stood up on the nursery mantelpiece.

He found a button off the soldier's tunic and he picked it up and popped it into the slit of the money-box. Clink! It fell in among the pennies and lay there. Then the Cockyolly bird hunted about for something else, and found the lamb's tail. It was always loose and had fallen off on to the floor.

The Cockyolly bird picked it up and flew off with it. He stuffed it into the money-box. Aha! The lamb wouldn't know where it had gone. He would look

The Bad Cockyolly Bird

for it all over the place.

Then the Cockyolly bird found the brooch belonging to the walking-doll. Dear me, he *was* pleased! He had once asked the walking-doll to lend it to him when he went to a party, and she wouldn't – so now she would be punished, thought the bad Cockyolly bird! He pushed it into the money-box. It fell inside with a little tinkling noise.

But the worst thing he did was to take the teddy bear's glass eye. The bear had two beautiful eyes, both made of brown glass, round and shining. But one was loose, and sometimes came out. Then it had to be stuck in again.

The teddy bear wanted to romp about one night, so he took his loose eye out and laid it carefully down on a chair in the doll's house. That was where the Cockyolly bird found it. He picked it up in his beak and flew off with it at once. Clink! It went into the money-box.

Oh, what a to-do there was when the teddy bear found his eye gone! 'I know that wicked Cockyolly bird has taken

it,' he cried. 'Oh, I know he has!'

The toys surrounded the Cockyolly bird and shouted at him:

'Where's the teddy bear's eye?'

'Where's the walking-doll's brooch?'

'Where's the lamb's tail?'

'Where's the soldier's button?'

'Aha! Oho! Where *you* won't be able to get them,' grinned the Cockyolly bird. 'They are all in the money-box.'

The toys stared at one another in dismay. In the money-box! Why, that was always locked – they would never be able to get anything out of that.

'Oh, you bad, wicked Cockyolly bird!' shouted everyone in a rage. The Cockyolly bird flung back his head and laughed and laughed and laughed. He did like to see the toys so angry. As he laughed, his key came loose, and suddenly it dropped to the floor. Clang!

In a trice the baby doll caught it up in her hand. She raced to the nearest chair. She climbed up it, she climbed up to the back. She jumped from there to the mantelpiece – and she ran to the money-box. She dropped the Cockyolly bird's key into the slit in the money-box. Clang!

Everyone stared. The Cockyolly bird broke into loud wailing.

'Kack! Kack! What have you done with my key? When I am run down I shan't be able to be wound up. I shan't be able to walk, or fly, or peck. Oh, you wicked baby doll!'

'You deserve it,' said everyone at once. 'If you put things belonging to *us* in the money-box, why shouldn't we put in things belonging to *you*! It serves you right!'

So it did. When his clockwork ran down, there was no key to wind up the Cockyolly bird, so he just had to stand in his corner and glare at everyone, and wish and wish that he had never been so stupid as to tell people what a good hiding place the money-box was!

When Mother's birthday came the children who lived in the nursery opened their money-box to get out some money to buy Mother a present; and dear me, *how* surprised they were to find so many queer things inside.

'How did they get there?' they said to one another. But nobody knew.

The Cockyolly bird got his key back.

The teddy bear got his glass eye back, and all the others got their things back too.

'And just remember this, Cockyolly bird,' said the teddy bear, as he stuck in his glass eye once more, and glared at the bird with it, 'we shall only be too pleased to put your key in the money-box if you play any more tricks. So behave yourself in future.'

And now the Cockyolly bird is as good as gold. He did get such a shock when his key went into the money-box – he doesn't want it to happen again, you may be sure!